REFUGEES

by Marty Erickson

BrightP◆int Press

San Diego, CA

BrightPoint Press

© 2020 BrightPoint Press
an imprint of ReferencePoint Press, Inc.
Printed in the United States

For more information, contact:
BrightPoint Press
PO Box 27779
San Diego, CA 92198
www.BrightPointPress.com

LIBRARY OF CONGRESS CATALOGING-IN-PUBLICATION DATA

Names: Erickson, Marty, 1991- author.
Title: Refugees / Marty Erickson.
Description: San Diego, CA : ReferencePoint Press, Inc., [2020] | Series: In
    focus | Includes bibliographical references and index.
Identifiers: LCCN 2019005408 (print) | LCCN 2019007802 (ebook) | ISBN
    9781682827208 (ebook) | ISBN 9781682827192 (hardcover)
Subjects: LCSH: Refugees--Juvenile literature. | Emigration and
    immigration--Political aspects--Juvenile literature.
Classification: LCC JV6346 (ebook) | LCC JV6346 .E75 2020 (print) | DDC
    305.9/06914--dc23
LC record available at https://lccn.loc.gov/2019005408

CONTENTS

TIMELINE

December 10, 1948
The Universal Declaration of Human Rights is adopted. It guarantees certain rights to people fleeing conflict.

1951
United Nations countries adopt the Refugee Convention. This document defines the term *refugee*.

March 17, 1980
The Refugee Act is signed into law.

| 1940 | 1950 | 1960 | 1970 | 1980 |

December 14, 1950
The United Nations High Commissioner for Refugees (UNHCR) is founded.

1975
The Vietnam War (1954–1975) ends. Many people are displaced after the war.

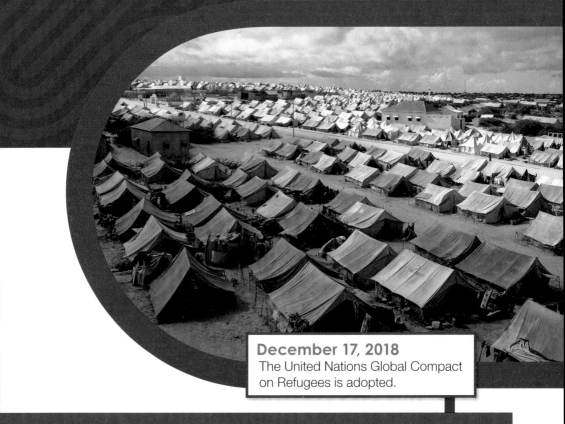

December 17, 2018
The United Nations Global Compact on Refugees is adopted.

1990	2000	2005	2010	2020

March 2011
The Syrian civil war begins. It displaces millions of people.

2017
The UNHCR finds that there are more than 68 million displaced people in the world.

SEEKING SAFETY

In March 2011, protests broke out in Syria. Protesters resisted the government. The government restricted people's freedoms. Many people were also upset about the high unemployment rate. Government soldiers attacked the protesters. Soon the conflict escalated into civil war. A civil war is a conflict between two or more groups in a country.

Many buildings were destroyed during the Syrian civil war. Some people are working to rebuild parts of Syria.

Soldiers bombed buildings. Many homes were destroyed. Millions of people were in danger. They needed to find someplace safe to live. They fled Syria.

Military tanks became a common sight in Syria after the civil war broke out.

Syria is a Middle Eastern country. It shares a border with Jordan, Turkey, and Lebanon. Many Syrians fled to these countries. The countries recognized them as refugees. Refugees are people who leave their home countries to escape violence or **persecution**. Governments give people refugee status. The United Nations High Commissioner for Refugees (UNHCR) can also give people refugee status.

THE REFUGEE CRISIS

Refugee status is a type of protection. Countries give refugees aid. The countries that bordered Syria gave Syrian refugees some protection. They set up settlements or camps. But they were not prepared for so many refugees. The camps and settlements were crowded. Conditions there were bad. Many Syrians wanted to escape. They looked across the Mediterranean Sea to Europe. Thousands of refugees crowded into small boats. Some crossed

the Mediterranean Sea to Greece. Others

traveled to the island of Cyprus. Their

journeys were often long and difficult. The

boats were usually overloaded with people.

Many boats broke down or flooded. Some

refugees drowned.

Many activists say the world is facing a

refugee crisis. By 2018, nearly 13 million

Syrians had become refugees. They were

one **displaced** group among many.

Activists are pushing for laws that would

make countries accept more refugees. They

also advocate for laws that would make it

Boat travel can be very dangerous. Refugees who travel in boats are exposed to the weather.

easier for refugees to cross borders and

resettle. They face a lot of opposition. But

their efforts may help countries be more

welcoming of refugees in the future.

CHAPTER ONE

WHO ARE REFUGEES?

Refugees leave their home countries for many reasons. They flee violence. Violence can come in many forms. Sometimes people face persecution. They may be targeted because of their race, religion, or participation in a certain social group. Or they may be targeted because of their **nationality** or political opinion.

Many refugees travel long distances on foot. They bring whatever belongings they can carry.

Their government cannot or will not protect them. Leaders make laws that do not recognize certain people as citizens. These people face discrimination and violence. There are no laws to protect them. They have no choice but to leave.

The most common reason people leave their homes is to escape conflict. Countries may be involved in wars. Sometimes these wars are with other countries. In other cases, they are civil wars. Many people

THE ROHINGYA

Myanmar is a country in Southeast Asia. In 2017, Myanmar's military attacked the Rohingya people. The Rohingya are Muslim. They are a minority group. The government considers them illegal immigrants. It denies them citizenship. The United Nations called the violence against the Rohingya a genocide. Genocide is the act of trying to kill an entire population of people. Thousands of Rohingya fled to Bangladesh. They do not have identification papers. This makes it hard for them to gain refugee status.

become refugees during a war. They
may flee by choice to escape the threat
of violence. Or they may be forced out of
their homes.

TYPES OF DISPLACED PEOPLE

Some people leave their homes but cannot
leave their country. They may not have
enough resources to escape. Someone in
this situation is called an internally displaced
person (IDP).

Asylum-seekers are also displaced
people. They apply for protection, or
asylum, within another country. They have
to be in the country or near its border.

They have to prove they are in danger if they stay in their home country. They might meet the definition of *refugee*. But they have not yet been legally recognized as refugees. They go through an application process. They may get asylum status. Then they can settle in the country.

People also have to prove they are in danger in order to gain refugee status. They apply to live in another country. They can apply for refugee status before traveling to the country. Refugee status allows them to settle in the country.

Thousands of Rohingya Muslims were displaced from Myanmar in 2017 due to violence and persecution.

DEFINING *REFUGEE*

In 1945, the United Nations (UN) was

formed. The UN is an international

organization. It is made up of 193 countries.

It works to solve human rights issues.

A UNHCR employee talks to people as they wait to enter a refugee camp in Macedonia.

Members of the UN met in 1948. They adopted the Universal Declaration of Human Rights. This is a document. It outlines human rights that should be guaranteed to all people. Among them is the right to seek asylum.

UN members met again in 1951. They talked about how to define the term *refugee*. They adopted a document called the Refugee Convention. The document laid out a clear definition. This allowed countries to determine who could apply for refugee status. Before this meeting, each country had a different policy. The Refugee Convention set a standard for UN countries to follow.

THE UNHCR

In 2017, there were 25.4 million refugees worldwide. But they are not the only people who have to leave their homes. The UNHCR

World War II displaced between 7 and 11 million people.

tracks displaced people. It is the largest

refugee agency. Refugee agencies help

resettle refugees. The UNHCR was created

in 1950. World War II (1939–1945) had

recently ended. Many Europeans had to

leave their homes during the war. When the

war ended, not everyone could go home.

Some had no home to return to. The

movement of so many people put a strain

on countries. European countries did not

have a lot of money after the war. Many did

not have enough resources to feed and

house all of the refugees.

The UNHCR was not meant to be

permanent. But the number of displaced

people kept growing. In 2017, more than

68 million people worldwide were displaced.

That included refugees, asylum-seekers,

and IDPs. About half of these people were

under the age of eighteen.

Today, the UNHCR tracks all data about displaced people. It also helps process applications for refugee status. Refugees can come from anywhere. But certain parts of the world have more conflict than others. People from Sudan, Syria, and Afghanistan make up more than half of the refugee population. These countries face a lot of violence from armed conflict.

APPLICATION PROCESS

The process of applying for refugee status is long. It takes between eighteen and twenty-four months. Refugees register with the UNHCR. This is usually the first step.

The UNHCR's headquarters are in Geneva, Switzerland.

But each country has a different application process. The UNHCR guides applicants through the process. It gives applicants information about the paperwork they need to fill out. UNHCR workers collect this paperwork. They interview applicants to learn more about them. The UNHCR finds

UNHCR workers help register people as refugees.

the best countries for resettlement. It works

with these countries' governments.

Some applicants resettle in the United

States. They go through another interview.

This interview is at a Resettlement Support

Center (RSC). There are nine RSCs around

the world. Then US security agencies

do background checks. They review applicants' paperwork and documents. They make sure applicants have not committed crimes. They also make sure applicants are not a threat to the country. Applicants go through health screenings too. People with certain diseases may not be able to enter the country.

Applicants who pass these steps are admitted into the country. They gain refugee status. Those who are denied entry cannot **appeal** the decision. But they can reapply.

The process can be longer for people who flee countries that do not recognize them as citizens. Governments do not give these people identification documents. The UNHCR must find other ways to prove their identity. This can slow down the process for months.

REFUGEE CAMPS

Most displaced people travel to nearby countries. Travel can be expensive. People often cannot afford to travel farther. Eighty-five percent of refugees go to developing countries. These are often the only countries that will take them. Developing countries are poor countries. Many people in these countries live in

More than 3.5 million Syrian refugees live in Turkey.

poverty. Turkey, Uganda, and Pakistan

have the highest numbers of refugees.

Developing countries have fewer resources

than developed countries. Developed

countries are wealthier countries.

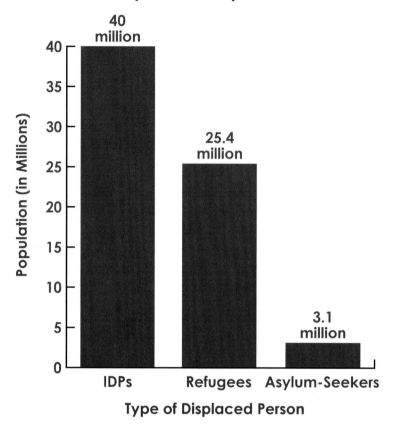

Displaced People in 2017

The above graph shows the population of displaced people worldwide in 2017.

The standard of living is higher in

these countries.

Some displaced people live in camps

while they wait to be resettled in a new

country. Others stay in settlements. Settlements are not official refugee camps. People in camps and settlements often live in tents. Living in a house could make it difficult to claim refugee status. A house could be considered a permanent home. People who want to gain refugee status in the United States cannot be permanently living in another country.

Camps and settlements often lack certain services. They may also lack certain resources. Health care is often limited. Some camps have temporary schools. The UNHCR partners with other groups.

They bring resources to some of these schools. The resources include computers and tablets. In many cases, the teachers are refugees. Some organizations offer training programs. The programs train people to teach in refugee camps.

Mohamad Al Jounde is a sixteen-year-old Syrian refugee. He and his family now live in Sweden. They fled Syria when Mohamad was a child. They lived in a camp in Lebanon. Mohamad built a school in the camp when he was twelve years old. Today, more than 200 students attend the school. Teachers educate the students on a

Rohingya refugee children attend class at a temporary school in a Bangladesh refugee camp.

variety of subjects. Mohamad said, "This is not just about teaching reading and writing but [about] giving young refugees a safe space to express themselves."[1] Schools are places where children can laugh and play.

This is especially valuable to refugees. Life

as a refugee is hard.

Displaced people continue to face

challenges after they leave camps. Shafaq

IMMIGRANTS

Some countries have high rates of poverty and unemployment. People flee these countries to find opportunities elsewhere. Many come to the United States. They can apply to get an immigrant visa. This visa allows them to live permanently in the country. The application process is long. It requires a lot of paperwork. It is also costly. These barriers keep many people from becoming legal immigrants. About 11 million undocumented immigrants live in the United States.

is a displaced person from Syria. She is fourteen years old. She lives with her family in Lebanon. She shared her story in an interview. She said, "We are living in a tiny house with one bedroom, a small kitchen and a bathroom. We are considered illegal because we don't have official documents."[2] Shafaq's family moved around Lebanon a lot. She had to attend a new school each time they moved. She was two years behind in school as a result.

CHAPTER TWO

HOW ARE ORGANIZATIONS HELPING REFUGEES?

Many organizations work with displaced people. The people who work at the UNHCR and other organizations want to help. The UNHCR is a large organization. It has offices in 127 countries around the world. It also has

The UNHCR supplies refugees with tents and other resources at refugee camps.

warehouses with supplies. UNHCR workers

give these supplies to displaced people

in emergencies.

The UNHCR has an office in the United

States. It helps refugees settle in the

United States. It aids them in the transition process. Other organizations also help refugees and asylum applicants. These organizations include Refugee Council USA and the International Rescue Committee.

REFUGEE AID

Refugees do not have a lot of money. They rely on aid organizations for help. Some organizations bring supplies to refugee camps. Supplies include clothes, food, and blankets. Many refugees are not able to bring their belongings with them. They need basic supplies. Other organizations give them medical care.

Red Cross workers serve food to refugees at a refugee reception center in Italy. The Red Cross provides aid to people in emergencies.

Refugees often settle in countries where they do not speak the local language. Organizations have translators to help them. These organizations give people important information. Websites such as Refugee

Info Bus and Refugee.Info direct refugees to country-specific aid. The information is translated into many languages. Refugees can read the sites in their own languages.

Lawyers help with the legal process of getting refugee status. This process can be

BOOSTING THE ECONOMY

Many refugees need to learn a new language. This can make it difficult for them to find jobs. Many refugees start their own businesses. For example, some open restaurants or grocery stores. They create jobs. They often hire other refugees. In these ways, refugees help grow a nation's **economy**. They give other refugees employment opportunities.

complicated and confusing. Lawyers help guide applicants through the process.

Applicants often cannot afford to pay lawyers. Some lawyers provide free legal aid. But they are busy. They get a lot of cases. There are not enough lawyers to help everyone.

Some organizations provide legal aid. One such organization is the Refugee and Immigrant Center for Education and Legal Services (RAICES). RAICES is in Texas. Many attorneys work for RAICES. They provide free and low-cost legal services.

Some human rights lawyers specialize in helping refugees and other displaced people.

EDUCATION

Refugees go through an **integration**

process. They have to adapt to life in a new

country. Education is an important part of

this process. Schools teach refugees new

languages and important skills. They also

provide a safe place for refugee children to learn and play. Refugee children can form new friendships.

Refugees can also learn more about their communities. Each culture has different customs. Schools and neighbors teach refugees some of these customs.

One refugee talked about trying to learn English when he arrived in England. He lived in a house with four other refugees. His neighbors were kind. He said, "They taught us about British culture."[3] Watching television also helped him learn English. He said this was helpful because

Syrian refugee children study in a classroom in Istanbul, Turkey, in 2015.

"the characters spoke in short sentences, [and] their accent was clear."[4]

Billions of dollars are spent on refugee services each year. But only about 2 percent of those funds go toward education. Schools for refugees often do not have many resources. About 90 percent of refugee girls drop out of school. Many are forced into arranged marriages. In arranged marriages, parents choose a husband for their daughter. The husbands are often much older than the girls. The parents may not have enough money to pay for food and clothing. Arranged marriages allow them to save money. The girls move into their husbands' homes. Then the parents no longer have to support their daughters.

RESPONSIBILITY TO HELP REFUGEES

Many people do not welcome refugees. Residents may resent refugees. They may think refugees take too much of the country's resources. This is the case in Lebanon. More than 1 million Syrian refugees live in Lebanon. There are not enough resources available in the country for all people. Some Lebanese people blame refugees for this problem. Some people destroy refugees' tents. They threaten to hurt the refugees. Syrians fear for their safety. One woman says the violence sends a clear message: "We'll host you while your country is at war. But don't think for a second that you're welcome to stay."[5] Many Lebanese people are against

There is not much housing available for refugees in Lebanon.

this violence. They say that lashing out

hurts everyone.

Filippo Grandi is the head of the UNHCR.

He spoke about how countries can share

responsibilities for refugee resettlement. In a

speech, he said, "Responsibility-sharing has been replaced by responsibility-shifting."[6] Some wealthy countries avoid taking in displaced people. They make up reasons to not give people shelter. These countries have caps. Caps are limits on how many refugees a country takes in each year.

WORLD REFUGEE DAY

The UN established World Refugee Day in 2000. This is a day to raise awareness about displaced people. One of its goals is to encourage people to be more accepting of refugees. World Refugee Day happens each year on June 20. The first World Refugee Day was celebrated in 2001.

Sometimes countries raise their caps when war breaks out in another country. They know more people will need help. At other times, countries lower their caps.

Grandi says that every country should help. Wealthy countries can give refugees more opportunities. Grandi thinks wealthy countries should accept more refugees. He pointed to local people helping refugees. Often, community members are willing to do what they can to help. Grandi said governments should follow this example.

CHAPTER THREE

HOW DO AMERICANS VIEW REFUGEES?

Not all refugees are treated equally when they arrive in a new country. Many countries are divided in their opinion of refugees. In 2018, about half of Americans approved of taking in refugees. Political beliefs influenced their opinions. Democrats were more

People gather in support of refugees outside the US Supreme Court in Washington, DC.

accepting of refugees than Republicans

were. Only 19 percent of Republicans

supported refugees.

Public opinion makes a big difference

in how refugees are treated. Many people

think refugees are not smart. One refugee

said, "I did not appreciate being talked

down to. . . . People thought that just

because I did not speak English, I was

not as intelligent."[7] Many refugees had

UNACCOMPANIED CHILDREN

Some refugee children are separated from their parents. They arrive alone in a new country. The United Nations International Children's Emergency Fund (UNICEF) helps children around the world. It protects children's rights. It provides kids with resources. It estimates that there were 300,000 unaccompanied refugee children in 2017. UNICEF wants countries to guarantee these children health care and education. In 2017, Italy passed a law. The law promises all refugee children health care and education.

A sign in the state of Maine welcomes refugees from Syria, Libya, Afghanistan, and other countries. Some US states are more welcoming of refugees than others.

successful careers in their home countries.

Others had been attending school or

university. But they had to quit when they

were forced to flee. They have to start over again in a new country.

LAWS

Politicians make laws that affect displaced people. In 1980, the US government passed the Refugee Act. The Vietnam War (1954–1975) had recently ended. Hundreds of thousands of people fled Vietnam. Before 1980, people were admitted to another country on a case-by-case basis. The Refugee Act created a standard. There was now a process for letting in refugees. It involved interviews and tests. The act also raised the US refugee cap. Before then, the

THE US-MEXICO BORDER

More than 6,000 **migrants** arrived at the US-Mexico border in November 2018. They were from Central America. They had fled violence in their home countries. They were seeking asylum. They had to wait in border towns such as Tijuana, Mexico. Some waited months before they got asylum. Others were not able to get asylum. Border stations use a method called metering. Metering only allows a few migrants to apply for asylum each day.

cap had been 17,400. The act increased the cap to 50,000. The act also allowed the president to let in more refugees during an emergency. An emergency could be a war or another type of conflict.

Despite the act's changes, the public's opinion of refugees was often not positive. The polling company Gallup surveyed Americans from the 1930s through the 1990s. The surveys showed Americans' opinions toward refugee groups. Many Americans disapproved of admitting refugees.

Each year, the president sets the refugee admissions cap. From 2000 to 2015, the number stayed between 70,000 and 80,000. President Donald Trump changed this in 2017. He lowered the cap to 50,000. He lowered it again in 2018 and 2019.

US Customs and Border Patrol officers patrol the US-Mexico border to keep people from entering the United States illegally.

The cap was only 30,000 in 2019. That was the lowest cap since the Refugee Act was passed. Trump called refugees a security risk. He believed they were dangerous.

REFUGEE RESETTLEMENT

The United States takes in refugees from all over the world. More than 15,000 Syrian

Central American migrants board a truck in Hidalgo, Mexico, on the way to the US-Mexico border.

refugees settled in the country in 2016.

The United States also has large

populations of refugees from Somalia,

Myanmar, Iraq, and Afghanistan.

Some people believe refugees are

terrorists. But research shows that

most refugees are not dangerous.
Three million refugees have settled in
the United States since the Refugee Act
was passed. Only twenty of them had
connections to terrorist groups. The
application process is an effective screening
tool. The process is long. This can
discourage some people from applying. It is
also thorough. Applicants go through many
steps. They must pass many background
checks and interviews. These checks are
likely to catch someone who has ties to a
terrorist group. People who have such ties
are denied entry into the country.

CHAPTER FOUR

WHAT IS THE FUTURE FOR REFUGEES?

In 2018, the UN adopted the Global Compact on Refugees. This is a **pact** among some UN countries. It calls for countries to work together to help refugees. Representatives debated the pact for more than a year. Countries recognized that there is a refugee crisis. But the world struggled

Flags outside the UN office in Geneva, Switzerland, represent UN member countries.

to find a solution. Officials estimated that

258 million people lived outside the country

of their birth. Not all of these people were

displaced because of violence. But there

are many who left because they were

not safe.

RESPONSE TO THE PACT

Of the 193 UN countries, 164 signed the pact. The pact left room for countries to make their own laws. It was nonbinding. It was more like a recommendation than a law. Countries did not have to follow it if they did not want to. That applied to all countries, even those that signed the pact.

VOLUNTARY REPATRIATION

Some refugees return to their home countries when it becomes safe for them to do so. This is called voluntary repatriation. The UNHCR and other groups help with this process. They take refugees back on "go and see" visits. These trips are important. They allow refugees to see whether it is safe for them to return.

President Donald Trump speaks at a UN assembly in 2017. Trump clashed with other UN countries during his presidency.

Not everyone thought the pact was a good idea. Some countries thought it would give them less control over their immigration laws. Others worried that they would have to let in more refugees. Countries are

Nikki Haley was the US ambassador to the UN from 2017 to 2018.

required to give refugees aid. Some countries thought they would not have enough resources.

The United States was the first country to pull out of the pact. Nine other countries later followed. Nikki Haley was the US ambassador to the UN. She said, "Our decisions on immigration policies must always be made by . . . Americans alone. We will decide how best to control our borders and who will be allowed to enter our country."[8]

Supporters of the pact say this is an opportunity for countries to work together.

Marta Foresti is a director at the Overseas Development Institute. This group works on human rights issues. Foresti was excited about the pact. She said, "[The pact] will help governments work together to . . . ensure that people making cross-border journeys can do so in a legal, orderly and safe way."[9]

OBJECTIVES

The pact has twenty-three objectives, or goals. One objective hopes to keep children out of detention camps. Detention camps hold migrants until their legal status is determined. One hundred countries allow

ICE DETENTION CENTERS

A government agency enforces US immigration laws. It is called US Immigration and Customs Enforcement (ICE). ICE can separate migrant children from parents in certain cases. In 2018, ICE separated more than 2,400 kids from their families. ICE put the kids in detention centers. Many people were outraged. Conditions in these centers were poor. The centers were overcrowded. They did not have many staff or resources. Between 2017 and 2019, twenty-two people died in these centers.

the detention of migrant children. This includes the United States. Some children are separated from their family during a border crossing. Others cross the border alone. In some cases, migrants may live in detention camps for years.

The pact also seeks to make legal border crossings easier. Illegal border crossings are often dangerous. The UN believes that if legal options are available, fewer people will try to cross borders illegally.

Another objective says no migrant should be forced to go back to their home country. This is a major policy change. Many countries send migrants back if they do not meet the requirements for asylum or refugee status. The UN pact says this puts migrants at risk. This is especially the case for people fleeing violence. One woman explained her experience. She was from

In 2018, people in the United States held Families Belong Together rallies. Families Belong Together is a group that works to reunite families and end detention.

Honduras. Gang violence is widespread

there. A gang attacked the woman.

The gang burned her arm with acid.

They damaged her left hand. As a result, four of her fingers had to be amputated.

The woman reported the attack to the police in Honduras. But the police did not do anything. She went into hiding for five years to avoid the gang. But gang members eventually found her. They threatened to kill her. So she decided to leave the country. She arrived at the US-Mexico border in 2018. An officer at the border turned her away. The officer said her case was not severe enough. The woman says she cannot go home. She does not know what she will do. She said, "I was hoping

In Mexico, Honduran migrants pile into a truck bound for the United States. Many people flee Honduras to escape its high rate of poverty and violence.

that the [United States] would give me

the opportunity to live with dignity. I'm not

asking for anything else."[10] A legal team

helped her appeal her case in 2018.

REFUGEE SAFETY

Louise Arbour is a lawyer. She works for the UN on behalf of Canada. She said, "It's not helpful to ask whether migration is a good thing or a bad thing. It's a thing, it's happening, it's always happened. It will always happen."[11] Instead of focusing on whether migration is good or bad, Arbour says countries should focus on making migration safer for everyone.

Refugees will continue to seek safety in other countries. As long as conflict exists, people will leave their homes. Some activists and organizations are calling on

Many refugee camps, such as the Atma camp in northern Syria, become overcrowded as the number of displaced people around the world increases.

Activists around the world are working to help others become more accepting of refugees.

wealthy countries to take in more refugees.

There is an imbalance between wealthy

and poor countries. In 2016, only 9 percent

of the world's refugees lived in the world's

six wealthiest countries. Activists believe

countries with more resources should be

able to take in more refugees. Activists'

efforts may lead to widespread changes in

the future.

GLOSSARY

appeal

to argue against a legal decision

displaced

forced to leave a home

economy

the exchange of goods and services

integration

the process of becoming part of a community

migrant

someone who travels from one place to another to find work

nationality

the status of belonging to or being from a certain country

pact

an agreement between a group of people or countries

persecution

the mistreatment of a group of people because of their beliefs or nationality

terrorists

people who use violence to intimidate or threaten others

SOURCE NOTES

CHAPTER ONE: WHO ARE REFUGEES?

1. Quoted in Kieran Guilbert, "Syrian Teenager Who Set Up a School in Refugee Camp Wins Global Prize," *Theirworld*, December 4, 2017. www.theirworld.org.

2. Quoted in Miranda Cleland, "13 Powerful Refugee Stories from Around the World," *GlobalGiving*, June 20, 2018. www.globalgiving.org.

CHAPTER TWO: HOW ARE ORGANIZATIONS HELPING REFUGEES?

3. Quoted in Mark Tran, "Refugee Turns Lawyer to Help Asylum-Seekers Rebuild in Britain," *UNHCR*, October 5, 2017. www.unhcr.org.

4. Quoted in Mark Tran, "Refugee Turns Lawyer to Help Asylum-Seekers Rebuild in Britain."

5. Quoted in Ruth Sherlock, "In Lebanon, Syrian Refugees Met with Harassment and Hostility," *NPR*, September 2, 2017. www.npr.org.

6. Quoted in UNHCR staff, "Grandi Urges Boost for Multilateralism to Tackle Record Displacement," *UNHCR*, October 1, 2018. www.unhcr.org.

CHAPTER THREE: HOW DO AMERICANS VIEW REFUGEES?

7. Quoted in "Refugees in Our Communities," *Welcome to America Project*, May 17, 2016. www.wtap.org.

CHAPTER FOUR: WHAT IS THE FUTURE FOR REFUGEES?

8. Quoted in Michelle Nichols, "U.S. Quits Talk on Global Migration Pact Over Sovereignty Clash," *Reuters*, December 3, 2017. www.reuters.com.

9. Quoted in Karen McVeigh, "UN States Agree Historic Global Deal to Manage Migration Crisis," *Guardian*, December 10, 2018. www.theguardian.com.

10. Quoted in Joel Rose and Marisa Peñaloza, "Denied Asylum, but Terrified to Return Home," *NPR*, July 20, 2018. www.npr.org.

11. Quoted in Megan Specia, "U.N. Agrees on Migration Pact, but U.S. Is Conspicuously Absent," *New York Times*, July 13, 2018. www.nytimes.com.

FOR FURTHER RESEARCH

BOOKS

Joyce Jeffries, *Who Are Refugees?* New York: KidHaven Publishing, 2018.

Sandra Neill Wallace and Rich Wallace, *First Generation: 36 Trailblazing Immigrants and Refugees Who Make America Great*. New York: Little, Brown and Company, 2018.

Steven Otfinoski, *Immigration & America*. New York: Scholastic, 2018.

INTERNET SOURCES

Joel Rose and Marisa Peñaloza, "Denied Asylum, but Terrified to Return Home," *National Public Radio*, July 20, 2018. www.npr.org.

"Stories of Syrian Refugees," *Save the Children*, n.d. www.savethechildren.org.

"Who Is a Refugee?" *RoadstoRefuge*, n.d. www.roads-to-refuge.com.au.

WEBSITES

Amnesty International
www.amnesty.org/en

Amnesty International is a global human rights organization. It raises awareness of human rights issues such as the refugee crisis.

The International Rescue Committee (IRC)
www.rescue.org

The IRC is a global organization that provides aid to refugees and other people in crisis. It helps people who have been displaced due to war, persecution, or natural disasters.

The United Nations High Commissioner for Refugees (UNHCR)
www.unrefugees.org

The UNHCR provides aid and other assistance to refugees around the world.

IMAGE CREDITS

ABOUT THE AUTHOR

Marty Erickson is a genderqueer writer living in Minnesota. Marty uses the pronouns "they/them/theirs." They write books for young people full time and like to go hiking.